Empowered By Disadvantages

WHEN YOUR DISADVANTAGES
BECOME YOUR ADVANTAGES

Lisa Ward

Empowered by Disadvantages

When Your Disadvantages Become Your Advantages

REVISED EDITION

By Lisa Ward

Front cover image by Guillermo Quirindongo.

Edited by FaLessia Booker, The Editing Expert.

Book set up: Jazzy Kitty Publications

Printed by Humble Doc Publishing in the United States of America.

© 2022 By Lisa Ward

REVISED EDITION

ISBN: 9781733030205

All rights reserved. No part of this publication may be reproduced, distributed, or transmitted in any form or by any means, including photocopying, recording, or other electronic or mechanical methods, without the prior written permission of the author, except in the case of brief quotations embodied in critical reviews and certain other noncommercial uses permitted by copyright law. Any names, characters, and places used in the stories are the product of the author's imagination.

First edition printing 2019 by Humble Doc Publishing. Email the author at lisaatward@gmail.com or visit www.lisaatward.com.

DEDICATIONS

This book and the new journey of my life are all dedicated to a couple of people. I first must thank my Savior, Jesus Christ for assigning this book to me. I never thought I could be an author, so I must thank Him for believing in me so much.

Thanks go to my baby sister, Frances McMillian, who always tells me I can do and be anything. She has been my rock for many reasons in this journey. To my children, grandchildren, and godchildren: I do this for you. You are the reason I keep pushing to be all I can be.

To Dr. Tameka "Doc" Wright, my right hand, I could not have finished this book without you. Our last months and days together were hard; but no matter how you were feeling (or I was feeling), you kept pushing me to write. There was a whole month when I didn't pick up my iPad to write anything. I remember you telling me I *had* to do this; I had come too far to stop.

I remember telling you, Doc, "If you're not here, I am done. We started these books together and we are going to end them together."

Doc knew I would do all I could to keep my word to her. She made me promise, no matter what happened, to complete my book for her. On Dec 10, 2018, I was done, exactly seven days after her birthday. The 10th day has many meanings and I know she is with me every step of the way because the number 7 represents completion.

To my parents, you gave me the gift of creation.

To my grandparents, you gave me the ability and the desire to want to help people.

To Amanda and Alina, thank you for standing by me.

To my team, there are no words for all you have done for me and with me. You all have a little of Doc in you pushing me and helping me keep my promise. So, a deep and special thank you goes to Dacia Almond, Angel The Poet, Jamil Bey, FaLessia Booker, Robin Brown, Françoise Campbell, Tammi Capri, BoB DeNiro, Nataisha Gales, Kimani Jackson, Rell Jerv, G. Jurel Jones, Randy McMillian, Barion McQueen, Shayla Parries, Guillermo Quirindongo, Aaron Rhines, Rollo Robertson, El-Rod, Malliki Saddler (AKA DJ Kaotic), Ex-Clavon T Simmons, Crystal Simms, Red Spade, Ira Spencer, Cynthia Talley-Wells, Kelz Tango, Michelle Waters, Lyrics Williams, Rachquel Winn, and Mz. Yola.

TABLE OF CONTENTS

Introduction……………………………………………………………..i
Chapter 1: Half My Story……………………………………………….01
Chapter 2: Childlessness………………………………………………..06
Chapter 3: Illnesses……………………………………………………..12
Chapter 4: Motherless…………………………………………………..16
Chapter 5: Success……………………………………………………...20
Chapter 6: Learning Disability………………………………………….23
Chapter 7: Pain………………………………………………………….31
Chapter 8: Fatherlessness……………………………………………….35
Chapter 9: Being Black…………………………………………………40
Chapter 10: Learning Never Stops within Life…………………………43
References………………………………………………………………46
About the Author………………………………………………………..48

INTRODUCTION

"God doesn't make mistakes."

That was the first thought I had as I sat on my bed and thought about how I could show readers of this book my passion. I decided to take my readers on a journey through stories that proved my points.

I once believed that being dyslexic was an unfavorable circumstance that reduced my chances of success until I developed a passion for writing which completely changed my circumstance and placed me in a position more favorable than I could have ever imagined. That's why I wrote this book. I want to help people embrace what they believe are disadvantages and learn to dissect them piece by piece; you may discover, as did I, that they are advantages that will change your life.

Life is like a game of chess. Before you can play, however, you must first understand the game. If you've never played chess, you must research the rules, the styles, and most of all, your opponents.

One of my heroes, Russell Simmons, stated that he is successful because he hires smarter people than himself. He surely would not have become the hip-hop icon he is today if he wasn't in the office every day, learning and recognizing the disadvantages and advantages of all the opportunities that came his way. Mr. Simmons is what you would call a leader. A true leader must first follow and then observe others. When you observe others and yourself, your advantages become visible. You also must look at your unfavorable circumstances and once you start to dissect them, you will see the truth.

I once worked as a consultant to a fashion company where the designer—young, super talented, and full of ambition—was new to the industry. I asked him, "Honestly, what do you think of your designs?"

He answered, "My designs are better than Sean John's."

While I admired his confidence, I didn't sugarcoat anything when I gave him my honest opinion. "You are not ready to be the C.E.O. of this company."

He asked both me and the owner why not.

I said to him, "Because you're not being real with yourself."

Once he looked deeper into what I said, he realized that he had not quite reached a "Sean John" level. Over time, with some hard work and dedication, he became an amazing fashion designer and an even better businessperson.

I pray that my message is truly a blessing to people who take the time to read it. I have gone years without knowing that my problem was my profit. So, you must open your eyes, and most of all your mind, to what is real. Once you do that, you will see that everything that life throws at you is not always a pitfall. The synonymous relationship between disadvantages and advantages will not only help you become the person you're supposed to be but could also help you save someone's life—maybe even your own.

CHAPTER 1

Half My Story

I grew up with three brothers and five sisters but always felt different because I did not learn the same way they did. Things came very easily to them so I would stay to myself because that's what was easier for me. I had my good and bad days in school, but then third grade approached. I was nine years old, and reading was not something I did very well. Whenever my turn was coming up, I would quickly skim through the book to find the easiest part to read so people wouldn't laugh at me.

I made it all the way to the eighth grade avoiding reading as much as I could. When my family asked if I had homework, I would say no, or that I had already done it. I have a very understanding family, so you would think my lack of reading wouldn't be a big deal, but it was to me. I wanted to be normal and like everyone else in my family, as well as in the world. I wouldn't allow myself to see the benefits that life had given to me.

All I saw were my drawbacks—maybe because I had a teacher tell me I would never be anything. It didn't help that the teacher was a white man. I had other teachers who were white that were very good to me, but sometimes it only takes one to break you for life. I was a kid that loved older people and never cared what color the person was.

One of my teachers, Ms. Green, insisted that I should enter a school district writing contest.

I kept saying to her, "No, I can't do that, Ms. Green."

And she would say to me, "Why not?"

I responded, "You know why. I can't read that well and you know I can't spell, so why would you make me do something I cannot do?"

"You can't do it because you don't want to," she suggested.

I started to cry, and she asked me, "Why are you crying?"

"Because you're my favorite teacher and you are trying to hurt me."

"Hurt you?" Clearly, she was surprised that I felt that way. "I would never do that. I am trying to teach you that you can achieve anything you want in life, but you must do two things. First, you must fight for the things you want. Second, if there is a wall in your way that you cannot knock down alone, then go get help to knock it down."

She sat there looking at me. I asked her if she was done talking to me and in return, she asked me, "Are you done with me?"

I had a look of confusion on my face. I challenged her, "If I do this, will you help me?"

Ms. Green said, "Yes, I will, but you are going to do the writing and research on the person you want the paper to be about."

I did as Ms. Green asked and she did help me get my paper done. What I thought would be something I would not like at all started to be something I enjoyed very much. I would work with Ms. Green during my lunch period and sometimes after school. It took me three months to write the paper.

I completed my paper the week it was due. I submitted my paper not feeling that great about winning the contest, but what I did walk away with was a love of storytelling and writing. Now, don't get me wrong; it was still hard to write. I needed a lot of help, which was a disadvantage for many years.

I still avoided a lot of things from time to time, but Ms. Green did one thing for me—she put a big hole in that wall that I had up in front of me. Once I had finished writing the paper, Ms. Green told me that I had the gift of storytelling, and if I would put my mind to it, I could be a great writer one day.

For many years, I thought Ms. Green was just being nice to me. I didn't believe that I could be a writer of any kind. So, what happened the next month I would have never imagined! The list of the people who won the contest was posted, which I was not aware was a national contest. My class, along with the whole school was called down to the auditorium.

As they were calling the names, Ms. Green said, "It doesn't matter if you win or lose. All that matters is that I wanted you to learn that you can do anything. I also want you to know that because your learning is a disadvantage to you, it could also be an advantage to others. Please promise me you will always fight for what you want and always ask for help if you need it."

I told her on that day, "I promise." The next thing I knew, my name was called along with ten other kids, and I was the only kid in my school district/city who won the national writer's contest. No one could believe it! From that day on, I kept Ms. Green's words with me.

It may have taken me a long time to write my first book, but what I did learn from years of working with many people of all ages, is that what we think is not always right. What I saw as a weakness and a disadvantage became my strength and advantage. Words are now my voice on paper, which I hope is a help to other people like me. If I just kept looking at what I couldn't do at the time, I would have never done that paper. If Ms. Green hadn't taken the time to push me, and help me, I don't know where I would be. I let a lot of things in my life pass by because of my disability, but I also never gave up. I kept my eyes and ears open to learning new things, and for years I kept looking deep down inside myself until I found what I was good at.

Now, look at me. I am talking to you through this book. Those who know me may say, "Well, that is *your* life. *My* life was hard, and you can't even imagine walking in my shoes. I was in a home with no one to teach me anything." I have another story for you to read as well, so open your mind, ears, and eyes when you read the next story.

There was a girl who was half black and half Chinese. She had parents who couldn't take care of her. She was only 16 years old with nowhere to go. She met an older woman who was like a mother to her, but no matter how much the woman showed the young girl love, the girl could never embrace the love this woman gave to her. She ran the streets doing all types of things that she was not proud of.

As she got older, she saw her life as a big mess that she didn't feel was worth having. She would stay with the older woman from time to time, but never long enough to feel at home. This young woman told herself that she was nothing, so why even try to be better? Before long, she was addicted to a drug called crack, which is one of the hardest drugs to ever break free from. We all know that this is an obstacle for many women of color.

Now, this woman has been clean for over twenty years and is a Christian. The disadvantages that took place in her life have given her the advantage of saving her own children and grandchildren from that same walk in life. She has won the biggest fight of them all, beating a drug addiction that normally takes the lives of so many people, especially black people.

Today, she is a happy woman with kids who have Christ in their lives.

Sadly, two of her kids fell into addiction, but all the kids are hardworking and doing their best to do the right thing. You see, her life of hardship was the tool that her kids saw as a lesson to not follow in their mother's footsteps. Some decided to change the generational direction of their mother. When the time came, she could look back and be proud of her children.

We all have a calling and a job to do in the Eyes of God. What our jobs may be is not always clear, but life is not a book of do's and dont's. We must learn and study our stumbling blocks in life and see what the blessings are in those situations. Once we see them, we can take them and use them to better ourselves.

You might even save someone's life after what you have experienced and learned. How do I know this to be true? I am that sixteen-year-old girl's daughter who lived life with what I thought were many disadvantages. But I now know that they were not disadvantages. So, for you to understand, I want to show you my life through my eyes and ears.

My mother's life gave me the tools needed to help people like her, but I would need to help them during their teenage years before they'd fall into the wrong hands. My mother's disadvantages were my advantages. Don't get me wrong—I didn't see it like that in the beginning. What child wants a crack-addicted mother? But if I had to do it over again, I wouldn't change the experience. It is the journey that God planned for me.

CHAPTER 2

Childlessness

Girls are told at a very young age that when they grow up, they will be great mothers. They are also told that they will make great wives one day. So, they expect to become mothers one day with great husbands. There is never any question that a young girl would not experience motherhood. Most parents' first gift to a girl is a baby doll. By the time they are teenagers, depending on the childhoods they have had, they are either looking forward to having children or despising the idea of it.

I never hear a parent ask a daughter if she would like to have children. What I have heard many times is, "You could become a single mother, so make sure you use protection or better yet don't have sex." Most mothers prepare their daughters for what would happen if their husbands/partners walk out on them, and they become single parents.

Parents rarely look at the possibility of something going wrong, like not being able to have children. Many young women are not prepared to hear their doctor say the word "infertility." All they hear is, "You can't have children." To some women, those four words are like being stabbed.

Many women feel that the job of a woman is to give birth, so when that is taken away from them, it feels as though they're no longer women. They now start to question who and what they are from so many angles. They start to feel less and less like women.

Infertility can hurt both the male and his partner/wife. The most common conditions of female infertility are endometriosis, premature menopause, anovulation (when an egg doesn't release from the ovary during the menstrual cycle), PCOS (polycystic ovary syndrome), uterine fibroids, fallopian tube damage, and low ovarian reserve.

When couples have tried to conceive for twelve months or more, they should go to a doctor to find out why they are not seeing a pregnancy occur. Society always looks at the woman first because male infertility is often neglected. Men don't talk about how infertility affects them because they are ashamed, and their male pride is wounded. Infertility, to some men, is a woman's condition.

There are seven conditions that can make a male infertile: pain and swelling in the testicles, known as scrotal swelling. This condition relates to the enlargement of the testicles. The second is a poor sense of smell. This might seem strange, but it could be a symptom of a genetic disorder called Kallmann Syndrome. The third is ejaculation disorder. Fourth is a low sperm count, one of the most common signs of infertility in men. Fifth, testicles that are smaller than normal. Low sex drive can also be a sign of infertility in men. Finally, in men who have gynecomastia, swelling in the breast tissue could signal an imbalance in the hormones.

When men discover that they are infertile, many of them go through depression, anger, regret, sadness, denial, and loneliness. Some men may act as if it were never mentioned to them.

Men who go through infertility also learn that there are very few support groups for men only. Many support groups are for women only or couples. Some men are more comfortable in a group of just them; that type of group would give them a safe place to be honest about their deep dark feelings about their condition; a place where they wouldn't have to "be strong" or openly emotional.

Since they don't have that safe space, some men will isolate themselves from their families and friends because they fear they may lose their wives/partners. Women, no matter what the news is, will usually be ready to communicate with their loved ones. Men tend to hold everything in because they feel they need to be strong for their women. This action that the men take is not good for them or their families. Men feel better talking to other men when they need to express feelings this deeply. Some men feel they are not real men, and then they hear, "It's ok, you can adopt." To most people who want children—especially men—adoption is not even an option at first.

Both sexes face a reality that they were never prepared to face. Infertility can be seen as a disadvantage to many people who may be unable to do what they think they were created to do on this earth. They cannot see anything good about not having children. But there is an advantage if we take the time to look at the journey we are walking into. We may have already been walking in the true direction that we were born to walk on earth.

Now, I know so many of you are saying that I am crazy. You think, "I am not going to read this nonsense;" but I promise you if you stay with me, you will see your disadvantage is your advantage. I would like to start with a story that no matter how many times it's told or heard, the impact is the same—everlasting.

At a very young age, Tonya was told she couldn't have children. She was heartbroken deep down inside. In her mind, a medical professional told her she was no longer a woman. Tonya cried for weeks, with only her parents knowing that dark secret in the closet that she never talked about much. As time went on, hearing her friends talk about having kids became harder to ignore.

Tonya had a group of friends that she grew up with who started questioning why she was not coming around to hang out anymore. When she started telling her best friends why she had stopped coming around as much, they were just as devastated as she was about the news her doctor told her. They held her, cried with her, and told her they would do whatever they could to help her with the situation.

Tonya truly appreciated the support her friends were giving her, but deep down inside she knew there was nothing they could do. They could not change her condition. Her friends could not understand how someone who was so great with kids could lose the ability to have kids. All they wanted to do for their friend was help her and take away that emptiness and pain she was feeling.

In time, they did help Tonya the best way they could—by keeping her around kids. One of her friends was a teacher and asked Tonya to volunteer at the school to counsel and mentor. She did take the offer since she loved working with kids of all ages. She became very popular among the kids in the school and the community. She was always the first to talk to the kids and the last one to leave at night. Tonya always made time for all children. Her relationship with the kids in and outside of her community was breathtaking.

Tonya's name also became very popular among the administrative staff and the police because of the volunteer work she was doing in the community. She was always called to speak at different events to show kids that it doesn't matter how you grew up because you can be whatever you want to be. Tonya was like Joe Clark in the movie *Lean on Me*. As time

Empowered by Disadvantages

went on, Tonya took kids into her home many times. She couldn't save every child, but she did help many.

Every week, she would go home and see this young man in her hallway dressed in his ROTC uniform looking very handsome talking to his girlfriend, even in the middle of winter. One day when Tonya came home, the young boy and his girlfriend helped her with her bags.

She thanked them both and asked, "Why are you always in my hallway?" They said that they used to live in the building, and they liked talking there because it was safe and quiet. She thanked the young couple and went into her warm house. She was impressed with the way they both conducted themselves, but the young man made a lasting impression.

One frigid Saturday, Tonya invited the young couple into her home. They looked at each other, then at her, wondering if they should go inside. They asked her, "Why are you being so nice to us?"

Tonya said, "Well, you have been in my hallway for over six months and it's too cold to be in a hallway. So come in and make yourself at home, but if I see or hear anything that should not be taking place, there will be consequences. Do you understand me?" They looked at her, smiled, and said, "yes."

That young man today is Tonya's son. Yes, you read that correctly! See, that young man didn't have parents; he lost them at a very young age. Tonya always tells people when she goes out and speaks that if she had been a mother biologically to her own children, she wouldn't be the woman who has taken in so many kids. She wouldn't have become a mother to a motherless boy who really needed someone to not only call his mother but to also love him with that unconditional motherly love.

Tonya also was blessed to have a daughter who she loves deeply. She was her first child, the one who went everywhere with her. Their relationship is amazing. They are not only mother and daughter but best friends. The love that she gets from her first child made it so possible to love and open her heart to her son. Tonya has always told her daughter she saved her life by allowing Tonya to be a second mother to her, which was life-changing to this day. Tonya always tells both her kids how God did an amazing job picking them for her because they have a lot of her ways. If she never told anyone you would never know they were not her biological children.

At first, not having children was a trial for Tonya, but it was her triumph. You never know the purpose of your walk until you walk it. Today, Tonya is blessed with three grandchildren and an amazing son and daughter of her own. The three couldn't be any happier with one another than they are today. They are each other's advantages and treasures.

CHAPTER 3
Illnesses

There are moments in our lives or in our family's lives when we are faced with the hardship of an illness that is chronic. You see, illness is something that we can't get past. Did you know one out of every three individuals has a chronic illness? There are many people who ask me, "How do you know if you have a chronic condition?" First, you must see a doctor to analyze any condition. A chronic illness is an illness that lasts three months or more. If your chronic illness is endometriosis, that is a condition that has many strange symptoms. The symptoms make you start to ask yourself whether tomorrow is promised to you. It's a condition that turns your life upside down.

There was a mother who at the age of 30 was faced with the condition of endometriosis. She had heard of the condition for about ten years, but never thought she would be faced with an illness that would destroy her internally. She was okay with the condition that would make it hard to have children because she already had three kids. All she wanted was the pain to go away and the bleeding to stop forever.

She was fine with having a hysterectomy. Most women are not happy about getting their reproductive systems removed. But, since she already had three kids, that was a no-brainer. She was so happy. She told the doctor to take it all. "I will be happy to have no more periods. So, the answer is YES."

I know at this point you are wondering why the person's name has not been mentioned, and that is because it is a story of many women. I'll give her the name Ms. Condition. All Ms. Condition wanted was the pain that her many cysts were causing to be removed. These cysts caused her to miss many days of work. She felt like she was pregnant and wondered if it was possible that she could be pregnant.

The symptoms associated with endometriosis are overwhelming for any female on a daily or monthly basis. This is a condition you wouldn't want to wish on your worst enemy! We must start looking at other options that will help us get through these types of illnesses. For example, we can use group intelligence: doing things that can help a person with an illness feel better. Here is an example of someone using group intelligence.

There was a woman named Crystal who was given the news that she had Stage 3 cancer and she was a book author. After getting the news of her condition, she knew she had to tell her publishing company and publicist of ten years. She didn't know how they would handle it. After setting up the meeting, she still had the support of the publishing company. They wanted her to get better and they told Crystal that she wouldn't want anything because they would cover her medical expenses.

"Just get better," they told her.

After that, her publicist's reaction was very surprising not only to her but to everyone in the room. You see, Crystal and her publicist were friends. She relocated her publicist after getting picked up by her publishing company. They had worked together for ten years as well. They did everything together. Crystal was the godmother to her child. She told Crystal she was very sorry and worried about her. She asked Crystal many questions such as, "What is your recovery time after you go through chemo?" and "How long would it be before you get back to work?"

At first, Crystal thought she was asking out of concern and friendship.

But that wasn't the case—she was asking because she wanted to know how long it would be before Crystal could go back to work. You see, Crystal had tour dates and appearances that had to be canceled, which meant no income for her publicist.

On that day, she walked out on Crystal, saying, "I am so sorry, but I must quit. I also don't want to see what you are going to become."

Crystal, with tears in her eyes, asked, "What do you mean?"

"You are never going to write again and if you do, you're not going to be the same. I see what cancer has done to people and I can't stay around for that. Goodbye," said the publicist.

So, which one do you think had illness intelligence? If you picked the first one, you would be correct. Crystal started to think that her life was over after her closest friend walked out on her. She started to think negatively, but her publisher helped her by asking, "Who are you? What have you been doing for the last ten years?"

Crystal had a look of confusion as the publisher continued. "You are a writer, a person who has written and spoken to many people. You have been encouraging so many people, so why would you stop now?"

The publisher asked Crystal another question. "Do you remember the movie, *The Five Heartbeats?*"

She said, "Yes, what about it?"

"Do you remember the part when Duck found out his brother and fiancée was cheating on him?"

Crystal was confused.

"Well, I will help you remember. Duck was giving his award acceptance speech. In that speech, he stated to the audience that he was told by his mentor that you become a great writer when you suffer more. Duck repeats the statement again, 'when you suffer more.' Duck states that he didn't understand at first, but he does now. He then thanks his brother and fiancée, who were cheating on him with each other. So, pain is not about pain but what you get from that pain."

As you see, when it came to Duck, his pain, which was at the time a disadvantage in his mind, was an advantage because with that pain he became a great writer.

There are so many people with chronic illnesses who might feel as if God is punishing them. But we must remember there is no happiness without sadness. We have people who have become motivational speakers about their illnesses. They have decided not to let their illnesses stop them. They have finally realized their illness is a sad thing, but not a total disadvantage.

If your journey is a journey of illness, did you ever ask yourself, why you? You were chosen because God knew he picked the right person to endure the journey of illness. God also knew that you would be able to help someone else who might not be as strong. You must understand that dealing with any illness on an everyday basis is very hard, but you can end up helping other people or by speaking at events. Your ability to fight back with an illness is the biggest advantage that a person needs.

CHAPTER 4
Motherless

When you think of the word "motherless," you have so many people saying things like, "How could she? I would have never left my child in the first place." Life has its way of making even the best mother do something that can sometimes come across as unforgivable, heartless, and even a disadvantage to one's life.

When you are young and realize that you are a motherless child, you feel all types of things inside. You are always wondering why your mother didn't love you or wondering what you could do to make the woman who gave you birth love you and be the mother you need. You start talking to God. You may not understand who He is, but you know people talk to Him when they need help.

For those who know who He is, the reaction may be different. They become angry with God in some cases. How could He allow this to take place? A child who is motherless might feel this would be a good time to ask God questions or have a one-on-one talk with Him. When you're young, you are thinking that you're going to get the answers to your questions, and when there is no answer from God or even from the woman who gave birth to you, it hurts. All you might have (if you are lucky) are some pictures and an official paper that is called a birth certificate with a woman's name on it that you don't even know. You become angry with life and sometimes with yourself. There are also times when you wish that the woman who birthed you had an abortion. You feel this way because why would you want to be a child who is motherless?

Kids who come from abandoned homes sometimes can see many bad things. The system is not always the best place for an unwanted kid to go, but our choices were taken from us when our mothers walked out the door to never return.

Yes, there are some great stories of kids being adopted. I am a big believer in good adoption facilities, but we can't be blindsided and think there aren't bad ones too. There are many horror stories as well. There are stories of kids being enslaved, beaten, raped, and even killed who were adopted or placed into foster care systems. One example is the Hart family, adoptive mothers who committed a murder-suicide while running from allegations of abuse and neglect, killing themselves and their six children. We need a better evaluation system for adoption facilities and foster care so these motherless kids can be safe and have a fighting chance for a wonderful life.

Being a motherless child is very hard and can come across in a negative light. It is very hard to see the good in yourself when in your mind your own mother didn't or couldn't see it. You can stay mad at the life you were handed, or you can take what your life has given you and see if there is anything good about being motherless.

There are times when we need to pick a path. But are we the one picking it—or is it a journey that was given to us from the very beginning of our birth and we just can't see it yet? For example, take the story of Mary, who gave her children up because she didn't know how to be a mother at the time. No job, no education, and a drug addiction didn't help. All Mary knew was that she didn't want to put her kids in the foster care system as her mother had done with her. Mary couldn't understand it because her mother had other children and she made sure to place those kids with family members.

Mary is the only girl who was placed into the system, and she didn't understand why. She would ask herself if it was because she was the only girl who was black that her mother had given birth to. After thinking about it for some time, she knew there had to be another reason that she couldn't get the full story from her mother. Mary's brothers were white, so their lives were better—no foster care for them.

Mary picked a path of sleeping with many men, looking for love. In her mind, it was love that she hadn't gotten since she was motherless. She was blessed to come across many women who wanted to fill that void, but Mary didn't know how to accept it on an everyday basis. When it became too much for her, she would run away and be missing for months. To Mary, her life was a disadvantage with no light at the end of the tunnel.

She felt that hopelessness until she got older. Then she realized that the path she was on had prepared her to be a fighter and to help other kids or women like herself. She even became a mother to a motherless child who loves her deeply.

The point I wanted to show in this story is that Mary's difficulties in her young life helped her to be the woman and mother she is today, not only to that motherless child, but to her own children and grandchildren.

Later, Mary got a second chance to be a mother to her own children after 30 years. Mary gets sad at times because she feels as if she failed them. Her life of disadvantages may have become her children's advantages, but they are also the strong women they are today because of her. There is always a reason for bad things that happen. Being in so much pain or so angry at the time makes it difficult to take the time to see the true purpose of it, and what can be learned from it that might be a help, not only to ourselves, but also to others.

CHAPTER 5
Success

One of the most popular questions I am asked by the youth is how they can find success like Drake, Chris Brown, Usher, Bow Wow, Mary Mary, or MC Lyte. I explain to them that success is different to many people and is misunderstood by many. So many people want to be successful but don't understand the pain and hard work that comes with it. There is no success without pain. Many people don't understand the downside that comes with being successful, things like not having the time needed to grieve the loss of a loved one. I have interviewed many artists, and some had to overcome the pain of being absent at the death of a loved one.

There was an artist who had a very hard life. He was homeless and did a lot of moving around. The love he had for his music and for his mother is what helped him get through being homeless. Because he was dealing with a life that was very hard, he developed a tough attitude that led him to trouble in school and to get into fights.

His mother decided to send him to live with his father. His father told him, "If you want to keep singing and doing this music thing, you better straighten up." He loved music so much that he got his act together because he knew his father wasn't playing. So, the young artist started working harder than he ever had. He got the chance to audition for one of those big shows on television like *The Voice*.

His mother was so very happy and proud, words couldn't express her happiness. The young man made it through the audition. But the young man's mother did not. You see, he lost his mother right at the time he was doing the show. That type of loss will break anyone. To him and many people, that loss was one of the biggest disadvantages for him to deal with. If you were to ask him, it was certainly a struggle, but it made him a better person.

He states that God doesn't make mistakes. So, to him, the hardship he endured when he lost his mother had become an advantage because everything he went through made him stronger and gave him more determination. He now sings with pain, desperation, and love. He makes people feel what he feels when he is singing. He can show the people those emotions because of the seeming disadvantage in his life that was more of an advantage.

It is very hard to see any good in death. But death was never supposed to be seen in the light of sadness. When people pass on, we are supposed to be celebrating the life that person had. But we all fall into our natural reaction of pain and sadness which is normal when you lose a loved one. What we need to remember is what comes after the passing of someone. That young artist has gone on to receive music awards, volunteered to help others who have cancer, and he feeds the hungry. He took his journey with his mother and turned it into something great for others. He remembers what it was like to not have anything for Christmas and not have anything to eat. Yes, the loss of his mother was hard, but he also knows that her loss is his biggest strength. She raised an amazing young man who knows how to push past the pain and see the light of that disadvantage. Being successful is hard on so many levels, like not being able to spend time to grieve with loved ones or missing your kid's birthdays or birth.

People like Michael Jackson and Usher who became successful while young have also had their share of disadvantages. Those disadvantages weren't all bad. They helped them become the great entertainers that they are for the world to see and become the fathers that their children can look up to. So, when you ask about being successful, you must understand that success is a journey of happiness *and* pain. If you are blessed to have it in any shape or form, then you will understand how to see the light in a difficult moment you might be experiencing. You must take the time to dissect that moment so you can come away with the lesson it was supposed to bring you. If you can do that, then your journey in life will be so much clearer and better when you're trying to find success.

CHAPTER 6
Learning Disability

Author's note: This was the most difficult chapter for me to write. I was diagnosed at a very early age with a learning disability. My family was only told that I had a problem with reading and writing and once I didn't pass the first grade, my family was advised that I needed to be placed in special education. To go through school in Special Education and not understand why I was put there was the toughest thing for me to deal with. Kids teased me every day; something like that can break anyone's self-esteem. It's even harder when you don't understand why you are different from everyone else. Often, I wonder why I couldn't read as well as my other classmates or why it was so challenging to keep up with what the teachers were saying.

Dyslexia is caused by relying more on Broca's Area in the left frontal lobe of the cerebrum. So, the logical processing problem on the left side of the brain affects analytic thought, language, science, logic, and math. But the trouble is not with seeing language, but with manipulation of it. For example, dyslexic people need to break words into parts so they're able to decode, read, and understand them. People with dyslexia have trouble connecting the sounds that make up words with letters that represent those sounds. The human brain was never designed to read and the ability to do so comes from the three parts of the brain responsible for sounding out unfamiliar words, recognizing familiar words by sight, and finally pronouncing the word.

Statistics show that thirty-five percent of high schoolers drop out because of a learning disability, fifty percent get involved with drugs and seventy percent become juvenile delinquents. These statistics exist because there is no real-world solution for people who struggle with learning disabilities.

Dyslexia is a hereditary learning disability, so if one of the parents has dyslexia, there is a 50% chance that their child will have dyslexia. As of 2011, dyslexia affects fifteen to twenty percent of the world's population. One in five people typically have difficulty reading or interpreting words, letters, and other symbols; for example, a dyslexic person may confuse small words like at/to, said/and, or does/goes. They may reverse the letters d and b, and read dog instead of bog. They may reverse words and read tip instead of pit, or substitute words like house and home. However, it does not affect general intelligence. The symptoms of dyslexia include poor short-term memory, concentration attention span, difficulties with organization and time management, and physical coordination, but the most well-known symptom is seeing words backward.

When I was in school, there weren't many people who truly understood the brain of a person with dyslexia. Today, researchers are using brain imaging to learn how it works with and without dyslexia. It's been discovered that if a dyslexic person can learn to enhance their brain activity, then they could possibly become better readers with that, researchers have also been studying the various strengths linked to dyslexia such as increased creativity. So, hope is out there for the development of more wonderful tools that can help people with dyslexia overcome their disabilities.

There is no cure for dyslexia, but help such as tutoring, speech therapy, and eye therapy is available. However, family support is vital to people who have a learning disability. The world is very hard on people like me, but there is hope every day. Two French scientists, Guy Ropars and Albert le

Floch, have discovered that dyslexia could be linked to a problem in the eye. While some researchers disagree with this finding, I personally have found this to be true because when eye therapy was introduced to me, it was a big help to me (along with all the other training I was doing to get better.)

How do eye spots confuse the brain? The Maxwell spot centroids in people without dyslexia are asymmetrical, which results in the person having a dominant eye—just like humans have a dominant hand. Having one dominant eye causes the brain to cancel out the mirror image shape. However, dyslexics have two dominant eyes which give the person a superimposed vision. Their brain tries unsuccessfully to process two of the same overlaid images. This can cause the brain to display a mirrored effect on the page, making it difficult to decipher letters and words. The brain doesn't know which letters or words to cancel out.

The Lili for life's lamp works to combat this by producing "imperceptible lights and flashes" that negate the mirror effect. According to the Jan 6, 2022, issue of the online website Reviewed, the Lili Life lamp has helped nearly 80% of users. The lamp has adjustable settings to find the optimal lighting for each user's unique needs. The lamp is also suitable for travel as well. For more information, please visit www.liliforlife.com.

Often, dyslexia can occur with other learning disabilities, such as attention deficit hyperactivity disorder, or ADHD. I was honored to meet with Kellen who has ADHD. He told me that he felt as if he had a social superpower. This advantage turned him into a social butterfly, and it is also why he can be so personable. Conversely, ADHD can be difficult at times because it can have a negative impact on the mental health of those diagnosed with it. Symptoms such as memory loss, poor time management, and anxiety can arise. As a black male, Kellen feels that having ADHD does make things more difficult because society already views black males in a limited way. The mental health of black males has not been taken seriously as it should be. He feels like it is harder as an adult, mainly because as a child he was not diagnosed with ADHD. Also, as a child, some of the behaviors that are a result of ADHD are already expected.

Kellen wasn't properly diagnosed until he was in his late twenties. By then, Kellen was already set in his ways. He didn't have a mental health issue to attach it to at that time because he didn't know he had ADHD. I asked him if he was concerned about passing ADHD down to his children. Kellen stated that he is not concerned about passing it down to his children because even if they were to have it, he will show them that it is manageable. He stated as their father, he can guide them through it. He would make sure to have them tested early in life. Remember he feels as having ADHD is a superpower that will help his children develop social skill that is needed in today's world. The greatest advice that he can give to someone that is like him is to remember to not allow people to define who you are based on your mental health. Your mental health isn't who you are. It is easy for people to attach what they know (or believe they know) about ADHD and yet again put you in another box. Don't allow it. The positive side that Kellen has experienced with his ADHD is that intelligence and common sense come as second nature. Most things he is challenged with are not difficult to solve for him. He thinks that is because of his hyper-focus, which is another common symptom of ADHD.

Many people with dyslexia, ADHD, or other learning disabilities quickly become overwhelmed and it's easy to take it as a weakness. Most of the time, that feeling comes from how they are treated by the public. How is it possible for them to conduct themselves in what's considered to be a normal manner when co-workers, classmates, and even loved ones constantly remind them of their struggles? Usually, it's not done intentionally, but most times they're blind to the harm they're causing. They speak to us in a demeaning fashion or overlook us for projects because they feel as though we're incapable of completing the task. If only they could walk in the shoes of a person with a learning disability for one day, their understanding and outlook would totally change.

One day, I was called into a meeting with parents who were totally against their son's placement in special education. This young man was the most disruptive student in the whole school. He was in the principal's office nearly every day and failed nearly every class. I believed his behavioral issues were a result of things not going so well at home and along with the issues he was having in school. When I first met him, we didn't get along at all, but as time went on, I was able to make enough of a connection with him that he would listen to me when he got in trouble in class. So, when I was asked to be a part of the meeting, I had no problem giving my input; in fact, I looked forward to it.

Once the principal gave his parents the options to either place their son in special education or be transferred to another school, they were so upset they said, "Give us the damn papers and we will be on our way!"

The principal replied, "before we do that, we would like Ms. Ward to speak to you because we feel what she has to share with you could be a great help in your decision."

I politely greeted them, "Hello, I am Ms. Ward and I work in the special education office. I understand your concerns, but I assure you that your perception of special education is totally off."

The mother angrily asked me, "What would you do if it were your son? Do you know how people would look at him? Do you have any idea how rough those classes will make his life?"

"Yes, I too was a special education student from first grade to eighth grade. I was blessed to completely be out of special education once I got into high school. But if I had to go through it again personally, I would. Your son needs this so he can get the help he needs to get better, not only in school but most of all in life. Special education classes, in my opinion, are always better no matter if you have a learning disability or not. I say that because the classes are smaller, and you can get more hands-on experience. You also don't feel rushed or out of place. You see when you are in a normal class the pressure that comes with that is overwhelming. Do you have any idea what it is like to have a room of people judging your every movement, laughing, teasing, and bullying you daily? Listen, I get it; it won't be easy and we're living in a very harsh world, but he's a bright kid. If you give him the support and tools that he needs his chances of success will go through the roof."

I know you love your son, but you don't understand the things we have to fight with. I am an adult now and I would not wish what I deal with daily on anyone, not even my enemy. I am always feeling like I must second guess myself or feel like what I am telling someone is not coming across the right way. I would ask myself if it were me or if it is the person I am talking to. Why can't they understand what I am trying to express? If that is not enough, what about if you are working at your job or doing a school paper and you hear the words you want to say or write down, but it doesn't come out the way you are imagining them to. I would cry myself to sleep on many days. There was even a time when I wanted to take my own life because I had no idea why I was not able to read or do my schoolwork like everyone else. I would lie to my mother about me not having any homework because if she was to help me with it and I didn't get it correct after her telling me something over and over she would hit me. So, I would lie about school. I know what he is feeling and what he is not telling you. Why do you think he is acting as he does in school? He does all these bad things to express his frustration of being misunderstood and not accepted."

"I had a teacher in this very school tell me I wouldn't be anything; that I wouldn't graduate or even go to college. That was one of my hardest days in special education because I wasn't sure if he was correct about me. The best day in special education was when my English teacher, Ms. Green, convinced me to enter a statewide writing contest that I ultimately won. If I had listened to that other teacher, I wouldn't be here now, I wouldn't have spoken at events, I wouldn't be the mentor I am today, and most of all I wouldn't have gotten a job working at the same school with that same teacher who must come to my office and deal with that same kid, who he told wouldn't be anything. Look at me now—I am in this meeting with you sharing my story.

I've talked to people of all ages and most of them felt as if their learning disability was a disadvantage. I know that is how you feel as well about your son. But take it from someone who was in special education, it is not a disadvantage, it's a necessary journey to help your son get to the next level of his life. It's a journey that pushes him to realize that what he has is not a disadvantage, but an advantage of a journey he did not see. I've spoken at many events to show that with hard work and determination anything is possible. I have also shown those who have treated people with learning disabilities that you shouldn't underestimate people with any type of learning disability.

Thirty-five percent of people who are dyslexic are entrepreneurs and forty percent of dyslexics are self-made millionaires! So, I ask you, how could a learning disability be a disadvantage when there are so many advantages to what I and many people like Albert Einstein, Whoopi Goldberg, Tom Cruise, Ervin "Magic" Johnson, Steven Spielberg, Steve Jobs, Tommy Hilfiger, Will Smith, Mohammed Ali, and Daymond John have contributed to the world and our youth? We could not have made the impact that we did if it wasn't for the journey we were given. So, I asked her to not hold him back from greatness; to give him the tools he needs to be the next millionaire. I know I said a mouthful, but the parents saw things my way afterward, and now that young man is flourishing.

CHAPTER 7
Pain

Pain affects many people, the one thing we would take back if we could. The hardest thing to see is a child who is dealing with an illness that gives them constant pain. Who wants to see their child in pain? No one. When we look at what pain can do to people, it is heartbreaking.

I know you might be asking yourself how pain fits within this book. There is no advantage to pain, most people would say. All people can see or focus on is the hardship that pain brings upon them. Now, please don't misunderstand me. Pain can be overwhelming to many people, especially cancer patients, women with endometriosis, phantom limb pain, emotional pain, or childbirth. Pain is one thing that most people want to avoid, if possible, but it is also the one thing that every human being will experience in life.

There are many ways to look at what pain is and where it comes from. Pain is an unpleasant sensation, an emotional experience whose purpose is to allow the body to react to damage. We feel pain when a signal is sent through nerve fibers to the brain for interpretation. The experience of pain is different for everyone. Pain can be short-term, long-term, or emotional. Physical pain can stay in one place, or it can spread throughout the whole body. According to the Oxford Dictionary, pain is physical suffering or discomfort caused by illness or injury. To the brain, pain is a part of the body's defense mechanism. It warns us to act to prevent harm or further issues.

What I want people to do is to look at their pain in a different light than normal. I have mentioned that everyone has a path in life. On that path, there are good and bad times. The bad times are things that we must face, including pain. So, pain is another obstacle or hindrance that we need to dissect piece by piece. To do this, I need to take you on another journey.

This story is about a football player who has been playing since the age of six. He is now playing for the NFL and breaking all types of records. The young man grew up in the projects and his parents didn't have much. He was the first to go to college on a scholarship. His parents were so proud of him. When he first started in the league, he would come back to his old neighborhood youth center and speak. He would spend hours talking to the youth about staying out of trouble and keeping good grades. He would tell them, "The pain you feel from an empty stomach or from a beating you got from the school bully because you didn't have the latest clothing, OK, it's only a moment."

He would tell them to take that emotional pain and physical pain and let that pain encourage them to study harder. Anytime they felt emotional pain, to take that pain and make promises to themselves to not stay in that emotional place.

You see, that is what got him to the NFL. To many people, his pain was a disadvantage, but he used it as an advantage to make a better life for himself and his family. What he learned from his hardships is that there is no journey in life without disadvantages. Try not to get stuck in that dark place where disadvantage lingers. The point of any disadvantage is to grow from the pain that comes from it. If you want to go deeper, read Matthew 25:14-23 New King James Version (NKJV):

The Parable of the Talents

[14]"For the kingdom of heaven is like a man traveling

to a far country, who called his own servants and delivered his goods to them. ¹⁵And to one he gave five talents, to another two, and to another one, to each according to his own ability; and immediately he went on a journey. ¹⁶Then he who had received the five talents went and traded with them, and made another five talents. ¹⁷And likewise, he who had received two gained two more also. ¹⁸But he who had received one went and dug in the ground, and hid his lord's money. ¹⁹After a long time, the lord of those servants came and settled accounts with them.

²⁰"So he who had received five talents came and brought five other talents, saying, 'Lord, you delivered to me five talents; look, I have gained five more talents besides them.' ²¹His lord said to him, 'Well done, good and faithful servant; you were faithful over a few things, I will make you ruler over many things. Enter into the joy of your lord.' ²²He also who had received two talents came and said, 'Lord, you delivered to me two talents; look, I have gained two more talents besides them.' ²³His lord said to him, 'Well done, good and faithful servant; you have been faithful over a few things, I will make you ruler over many things. Enter into the joy of your lord.'"

So, you see, the young man in Matthew didn't know the outcome of his journey: he was faithful with what was given to him and the outcome was better than he could imagine.

Another result of ongoing physical pain is that you grow to understand how pain can stop you from doing normal things like riding a bike, driving, going to the movies, or sitting in a chair. If you can no longer do those things, it gives you a higher respect for what a person can and can't do anymore. So, the advantage that my friend sees is that she can now help someone who might not understand what a person in pain deals with daily, or she can give an understanding of things that cannot be controlled.

If you are a person with pain, you must think about the simplest things now. If you go on a trip with someone, you must plan everything out so it can be more of a joyful trip than an agonizing one. The advantage to having pain is being able to be more understanding and to show empathy to others, and that is the biggest advantage of them all.

CHAPTER 8

Fatherlessness

Doc and I were at a high school event in September 2017, speaking about what is needed to be a recording artist today. After the event, there was a 28-year-old woman who asked to speak to Doc and me about her son.

We said, "Sure, have a seat. How can we help you, Ms. Spencer?"

She said, "Well, my friend told me you've made a great impact on her daughter Linda, and that you might be able to do the same with my son.

I said, "Yes, Linda is a sweetheart. Are you friends with the family?"

She said, "Yes, I am."

I replied, "Well, tell us about your son and what is going on that you feel we could be of some help."

Doc said, "You look so familiar to me."

I interjected and said, "You're right, Doc. Do you work at the hospital, Ms. Spencer?"

She said, "No, but I have been to a couple of your events. I really enjoyed your album release party. To see what you did for those young people was amazing to me. When my friend Tasha told me to talk to you, I thought it was a great idea. That is why I am here today."

I said, "First, Doc and I thank you for the kind words and appreciation for our work in the community." Doc asked Ms. Spencer to tell us about her son.

She said, "Well, his name is Michael. He is 15 years old and his father is not in his life. There was a Father and Son basketball game last month and ever since then, Michael has not been the same. You see, Michael loves basketball and he is very good. There are many colleges interested in him already. So, of course, when the Father and Son game came around, everyone knew he would be there. That is when all the questions started about why he did not play. It seems as if all the questioning took him to a dark and unfamiliar place. That is when he started cutting classes and not helping around the house like he normally does. He has been staying away from us and more to himself. That is not my son, and every time I ask him to talk to me, he says I wouldn't understand. One day, I was picking up his clothing off the floor in his room to wash it. As I was doing so, I saw his journal on his desk in his room, so I read it."

I looked at Doc and then I turned back to Ms. Spencer and asked, "What did it say?"

Ms. Spencer said, "It was a letter to his father, surprisingly asking him questions like why he didn't love him. What did he do so wrong to make him turn his back on him and me? Does he have any idea what it feels like to have something missing from your life? Why weren't you here in my life so we could be in the Father and Son basketball game?"

"Ok." I stopped Ms. Spencer. She looked at me with a look of confusion and tears in her eyes. I explained to Ms. Spencer that we had a clear picture of what she and her son were dealing with. I told her that we might be of some help. I saw how painful it was for her to tell us what she came across in his journal. So, I didn't want to subject her to any more pain since we understood what he was dealing with. I also told her that we might have to tell her son that she read his journal. "We will only bring that up if we can't make any breakthrough with him. But I am sure we will, Ms. Spencer. I will tell you that these feelings didn't come overnight. They were waiting for something to tip it over and that was the Father and Son Game."

This issue is not as uncommon as people might think. What Michael felt is not new and is normal. Being a fatherless child is an overwhelming thing for any person to deal with. When we come across a fatherless child, we really don't know the impact this child is dealing with from day to day. America is facing a fatherless crisis and most people have no idea how bad it really is. There are over 18 million children, which means more than 1 in 4 kids, who are living without fathers.

Also, according to U.S Census Bureau research, when a child is raised in a fatherless home, he or she can be affected in many ways. A daughter who is fatherless is more likely to be in an abusive and neglected relationship, become pregnant as a teenager, have behavioral problems, or abuse drugs and alcohol. Black boys are more likely to have behavioral problems that can land them in jail. They can end up doing drugs and alcohol or end up neglecting their relationships overall. Most of all, black boys can end up repeating the same cycles with their children.

There are disadvantages that come with being fatherless: so many young people and their families are destroyed. Young men may feel as if they must become their mothers' protectors since their fathers are not only missing from their lives, but also from their mothers.

Doc told Ms. Spencer, "Your son feels that if he opens to you about his feelings on being fatherless, it will add pressure that you don't need. Your son loves you very much but is hurting as well. He is trying to deal with his pain and trying to do right by you."

Ms. Spencer responded, "I don't need him to protect me. I need to protect him."

I said, "Well, see that is the issue right there."

Ms. Spencer looked at me and said, "What do you mean, Lisa?"

"You both need to understand that you can't really protect each other from a journey that you must take. You can support each other, but the journey that was created for you is something you can't stop. But most of all, why would you want to? We are always able to see the bad in things. We hold on to the pain that comes with all things, most of all our disadvantages. Pain seems to be the hardest thing to let go of or see anything good in it. So, yes, I think we can be of help to Michael as well as you."

Ms. Spencer answered, "That is great that you can help my son, but I am lost. Help me, how?"

I said, "What is happening to your son is also happening to you as well, Ms. Spencer, in a different way. You don't see it. Michael is going to need all of us to help him to see the advantages that are coming from his disadvantages. If he is open, then we can be of great help to him seeing his true purpose in life. You are taking the time to be a part of this, Ms. Spencer, and that will also help you find your true journey as well. You will also learn things not only about your son, but also yourself.

"This fatherless issue that your son Michael is facing is also your personal journey and disadvantage. We are going to help you dissect this disadvantage, piece by piece. In the end, you will walk away with an understanding of the advantage that comes out of this disadvantaged journey that you are on. So, when I asked you earlier why you would want to stop the journey that was created for you, it was for that reason.

"Life has many journeys, some good and some bad. But our journeys help us become the people we are today. We as people want to be upset and angry at the things that give us pain. We never want to stop and look at what we can learn or take from this pain that we are facing at that time. We don't want to see how a disadvantage can be a help to us in life overall. We as people must start opening our eyes and minds so we can get the real purpose of the disadvantage. If we stop and take the time, we will find the advantage. Once we find out what the advantage is, not only will we be helping ourselves, but we can then help others. But the real purpose is also to put you on that right journey that was already created for you."

We did have many meetings with Michael and his mother. Michael ended up doing fine. He is now helping other young people. He also now sees the advantage that came from being fatherless. He is not angry anymore. He found that talking about his feelings did help him deal with them better. We don't see Michael and his mom as much as we used to, which is okay. He is on a better path of understanding that his pain wasn't there to break him, but to lead him to a newer life.

CHAPTER 9

Being Black

Being Black is still an everyday stereotype in 2022. I am in my late 40's and I wish I could say as an African American that it has gotten easier. In some cases, it has. People like our grandparents, Malcolm X, Dr. Martin Luther King Jr., Jesse Jackson, Rosa Parks, Al Sharpton, Michelle Obama, and former President Barack Obama, to name a few, have done so much for us as a community and country. However, I hope you know that they had to face many disadvantages.

Malcolm X saw his father killed. He grew up in a time when being black was painful to so many. So, Malcolm saw being black as a disadvantage in his younger days, and he did things to fit in with the same race that almost destroyed him. He gave his life up for us. All you might see is the struggle with limitations. But when Malcolm goes to jail, that is the beginning of his realization that his life was not a disadvantage. With some help, Malcolm learned to see the advantages that came from his hard journey. All the bad things that happened to Malcolm happened for a much greater reason. The events that took place led him to become one of our people's greatest leaders; a leader that gave and still does inspire hope, power, dreams, and faith. He showed us as a culture that we were smart, strong, and can do anything that we put our minds to. Malcolm showed us how to stand up for ourselves and our culture. He also showed us that all races are not bad. Malcolm showed us that Blacks as a culture need to work together and be united to make a change that can be everlasting. Malcolm X's life of disadvantage was not only his advantage but also America's advantage.

Dr. Martin Luther King, Jr. was a preacher who stood up for what was

Empowered by Disadvantages

right. He did not know his life would take him down a road where he would be beaten and put in jail. He knew being black was hard, but if he could take what he learned from the Good Book—The Bible—and show our people how to handle violence with non-violence, maybe he could make a difference. Dr. King took a disadvantaged course of being in jail and being beaten. He replaced those disadvantages with the advantages of prayer, meditation, and meetings so he could help his people. In time, Dr. Martin Luther King, Jr. did so many things for his people and his country. We are still standing strong as a nation based on one of his greatest speeches, "I Have A Dream."

With the great sacrifices of people like our great-grandparents, Malcolm X, Dr. Martin Luther King, Jr., Rev. Jesse Jackson, Rosa Parks, and Rev. Al Sharpton, we were blessed to see the first African American man, Barack Obama, become the 44th President of the United States. Mr. Obama's whole election campaign was the beginning of seeing all our culture's disadvantages become our great advantage. Former President Barack Obama was the best person for the job because he was biracial. He could understand Black and White issues and bring the truth to Dr. Martin Luther King Jr.'s words: "I have a dream that one day this nation will rise up and live out the true meaning of its creed: We hold these truths to be self-evident, that all men are created equal."

America's 44th President's election was the first time I saw people of all races come together as one for a better world. He was what America needed to bring unity that had been missing for many years. If we can't take the time to see the good that came from centuries of pain, then we just don't want to see it. Obama was a man who took time to look at things around him to see if he could find the answers or the reasons why those things could be happening. Since he was able to learn from bad situations, he looked at those disadvantages and dissected them piece by piece to find their advantages. He ran America for eight years and should be looked at as one of the best presidents ever to run this country with eyes that were truly open to humanity.

CHAPTER 10
Learning Never Stops within Life

As I was writing this book, each chapter was something that I had seen God create, or that I had lived or personally experienced. I knew that every story I was sharing with you needed to be used. I used them because I personally learned something from them or saw others learn the lessons that they were meant to walk away with. I thought my journey was finished and that was why God gave me this book to do. This walk and these chapters had been completed in my life. I never thought my first book would be a self-help motivational book that is an enlightenment of understanding the roots behind your disadvantages. God gave this book to me to give to you the people. I never saw or thought I would have to reuse the tools in the book to overcome the hardest day of my life. This topic that I had to reencounter caused me to use my own book and tools to help me.

I touched on this same painful topic earlier in the book, not knowing I would be facing this issue myself. I wanted to overcome the pain and misunderstanding of the recent loss of my loved one. I had to use my own book to help me see the advantage within this disadvantage that I am now facing. When your loved one is ill, all you want to do is take the pain away or help that loved one to get better. When you are in it, sometimes you don't want to see the bad outcome; you want to believe or see that God is going to help your loved one overcome the illness or problem.

My good friend said to me, "Sometimes when you fight, you still lose."

I didn't understand what she meant at the time, but I do now. In life, we can fight as hard as we want to, but the outcome is already written. The paths that we must take, good and bad, are already lined up for us. What we must do after the pain has subsided and our minds are a little clearer, is to see the true picture of what our journeys are, and to find the advantages in these hard situations.

Doc was my right hand, and I needed to know what the advantage was in taking her from us so soon. She was facing an illness called multiple myeloma, which is cancer that has no cure, but you can live many years with it once it goes into remission or a transplant is done. The doctors were very positive that Doc would beat it.

Doc touched so many people. They said she was the most positive sick person they had ever met and the most requested. She would post positive things on Facebook and write her book at the same time. She was doing all these things sitting in the hospital with a weak body but a strong soul. That didn't stop her from believing, fighting, and, most of all, telling people who God is. My friend was the Rocky Balboa on her hospital floor with the help of an amazing staff.

As time went by, she was getting better because the cancer was at a standstill. However, what we thought was her comeback was really her final-goodbye to us from the person we knew and loved. What I did learn from this tragedy was that my past journey of disadvantages would become my future advantages. I know you might be wondering how my past helped me in my future.

I had an amazing grandmother who was sick when I was young. I had taken care of her for many years with the help of my father. I was 14 years old and helping my grandmother. I got my first job to make sure I could help her keep food on our table. I would go to doctors' appointments with my grandma. Because of her different illnesses, I was by her side for many days. When I was young, I did those things because it was the right thing to do, but I did not like it. I would talk under my breath like any other kid would do. I never knew the things I went through with my grandmother would be the necessary tools for taking care of my dear, dear family member today. I lost my grandmother at the age of 30. It is a day I will never forget. The hardest part about that day was I was not with her. I got there too late. I did get the time to sit with her, but deep down I always felt if I had to do it over, I would have been there.

What I got from my grandmother's illness and her passing away was the compassion, patience, and love to be by my family member's side today. I needed to make sure she had no worries. My family member was the one person who gave me the world and I wanted to be able to do the same for her. What I want people to walk away with is an understanding that everything we do is a journey with a lesson. We cannot be so closed-minded that we cannot see that. People are quick to see the negativity but so slow to see the positivity.

Each day that goes by is hard because at times it comes across as a repeat of a past disadvantage in my life. The two women who helped me be the woman I am today are now gone. I feel as if they created this strong woman who, because of them, will not give up, but they will not see who and what I have become. I know spiritually that they can see me, but the human side of me would like them to be here physically. Many of you might feel the same way about someone you have lost, but please know that we must keep pushing, and keep fighting. There is always a reason for what happens to us in life. We must always remember that learning never stops because we are still living human beings on a journey that has yet to be completed.

References

British Dyslexia Association. "See dyslexia differently." (Feb 11, 2018). Retrieved from https://youtu.be/11r7CFlK2sc Exceptional Individuals.

"What is dyslexia - what is neurodivergence?" (May 25, 2018). Retrieved from https://www.youtube.com/watch?v=cuZ7uPa0fsY

FRANCE 24 English. "Science: is dyslexia linked to eye spots that confuse the brain?" (Feb 7, 2022).

Retrieved from https://youtu.be/BMeMJpiz8mI

Holcombe, Madeline and Augie Martin. (2019). "Jennifer Hart drove her six children to their deaths as her wife looked up how much they would suffer, a jury says | CNN.

Retrieved from https://www.cnn.com/2019/04/06/us/hart-family-crash-inquest-searches/index.html

Le Floch, A., & Ropars, G. (2017). Left-right asymmetry of the Maxwell spot centroids in adults without and with dyslexia. Proceedings. *Biological sciences*, 284(1865), 20171380. https://doi.org/10.1098/rspb.2017.1380

Remarkable Minds. "Reading & the dyslexic brain." (April 12, 2022). Retrieved from https://www.youtube.com/watch?v=wUDZpmrZfz8

Sandman-Hurley, Kelli. "What is dyslexia?" (Jul 15, 2013). Retrieved from https://www.youtube.com/watch?v=zafiGBrFkRM

Schumacher, J., Hoffmann, P., Schmäl, C., Schulte-Körne, G., & Nöthen, M. M. (2007). Genetics of dyslexia: the evolving landscape. Journal of medical genetics, 44(5), 289–297. https://doi.org/10.1136/jmg.2006.046516

Skill Boosters. "What is Neurodiversity?" (Jun 27, 2022). Retrieved from https://youtu.be/GLGLLylcDvM

U.S. Census Bureau. "Living arrangements of children under 18 years old: 1960 to present." (2021). Washington, D.C.: U.S. Census Bureau. Retrieved from https://www.census.gov/programs-surveys/cps/data-detail.html

ABOUT THE AUTHOR

Lisa Ward is a motivational speaker, published author, manager, artist developer, mentor, and founder of Avodgy Collection, Humble Doc Publishing, and Deadline Production/management. *Empowered by Disadvantages* chronicles the ways that her adversities propelled her to the many successes in her life, such as establishing *SECDUM Magazine*, a publication featuring interviews of iconic artists. Lisa is also passionately dedicated to transforming today's youth into successful entertainers, entrepreneurs, and authors.

Ms. Ward gets her love for the entertainment industry, writing, and business hustle from her parents and her sisters. She is the second oldest sibling of nine creative and gifted children. She has accomplished a great deal in 36 years.

Lisa has always loved working with children and young adults. God changed Lisa's life and direction—He transitioned her gifts toward impacting the youth. Lisa helps young people develop their business careers and opens their eyes to the motivation behind their hardships. Keep your eyes on Lisa Ward and support her because whatever goal or project she sets her mind to, she will accomplish it and help as many people as she can!

www.ingramcontent.com/pod-product-compliance
Lightning Source LLC
Chambersburg PA
CBHW052120070526
44584CB00017B/2566